# ON THE RIVERFRONT

## Ottumwa, Iowa
*From Turkey Island to the Mixmaster*

Leigh Michaels
Michael W. Lemberger

Illustrations from
the Lemberger Collection

PBL Limited
Ottumwa, Iowa

On the Riverfront

This edition published 2014

10  9  8  7  6  5  4  3  2  1

ISBN  1892689510
ISBN 13: 9781892689511


Printed in the United States of America

Illustrations courtesy of **The Lemberger Collection**. For more information about the collection, which has been called the largest and best-documented privately-owned photography collection in the world, visit www.mlemberger.com.

Visit our website at www.pbllimited.com for more information about this and other publications. Quantity and wholesale prices are available.

# ON THE
# RIVERFRONT

# LOUIS VILLE

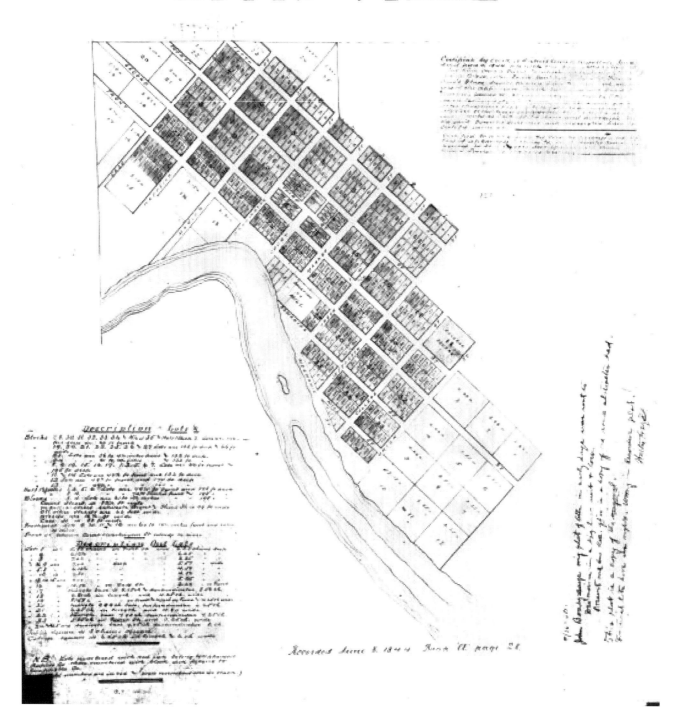

# THE CITY AND THE RIVER

Before the opening of Iowa to settlement, the bend in the Des Moines River where Ottumwa would later be built was home to several villages headed by Native Americans -- Chief Wapello and Chief Appanoose among them. Where a river bends, the flow of the water slows, making the location an inviting one.

Settlers from the East agreed, and Ottumwa -- originally Louis Ville -- was one of the first towns established when this section of Iowa was opened for development. Through the years, the river has defined the town. It has provided water for drinking, manufacturing, food production, and recreation. It has shaped the landscape -- dividing north from south until bridges were built, defining neighborhoods through repeated flooding.

More than 150 years later, the river remains the heart of Ottumwa.

This book is a companion to a slide show of historic images of Ottumwa's riverfront development, created as a public service project for Bridge View Center and the Home Expo of 2014. We wish to thank Larry Gawronski and the board of the Bridge View Center for their inspiration and support in developing the slide show and subsequent book, as well as Cheryl Cox and Dale Uehling for their help in final proofreading.

---

*Left*: Map of Louis Ville, Iowa, issued in June 1844 – just one month after the town was established. It was renamed Ottumwa about eighteen months later. This region of Iowa had been opened for development just a year before the town was founded. The bend in the river at center left is the site of Bridge View Center. The long island is Appanoose Island, which later vanished. College Square, located at center right, was set aside in the original settlement for schools. The site of the first school building in the city, it is the current location of Ottumwa High School.

This 1876 photograph is believed to show the original dam across the Des Moines River,
just upstream from Ottumwa. The dam was built of logs and is
still under construction in this view.

No man ever steps in the same river twice,
for it's not the same river and he's not the same man.
--Heraclitus

Map of downtown Ottumwa, 1875. Appanoose Island appears larger than in the earlier map. The first bridges across the river – Market Street and the railroad – are in place. South Ottumwa is starting to develop and streets and neighborhoods have been added on the north side.  Main Street is still known as Front Street. The original school building stands on College Square. The school, not named when it was built, was later called Adams School. It was replaced in 1883 by a second Adams School in the same location. College Square is the current site of Ottumwa High School.

Looking south from the tower of the new courthouse building in the early 1890s, showing the sweep of the river. The original river channel – what is now the lagoons in Ottumwa Park -- curves around through South Ottumwa and under the Market Street Bridge (the water flows from the right side of this photo to the left). Court Street is at lower right. The current site of Hotel Ottumwa is in the lower foreground, where several multi-story buildings stand in this view.

What makes a river so restful to people
is that it doesn't have any doubt –
it is sure to get where it is going,
and it doesn't want to go anywhere else.
--Hal Boyle

If one morning I walked on top of the water across the Potomac River,
the headline that afternoon would read:
'President Can't Swim.'
--Lyndon B. Johnson

A closer view from the same perspective shows the site of Bridge View Center, in the low-lying marshy land just to the left of the Market Street Bridge. The current site of the Beach is just out of the photo to the right. South Ottumwa has spread out along the far bank. Old St. Patrick's Church and Irving School are visible at far top right.

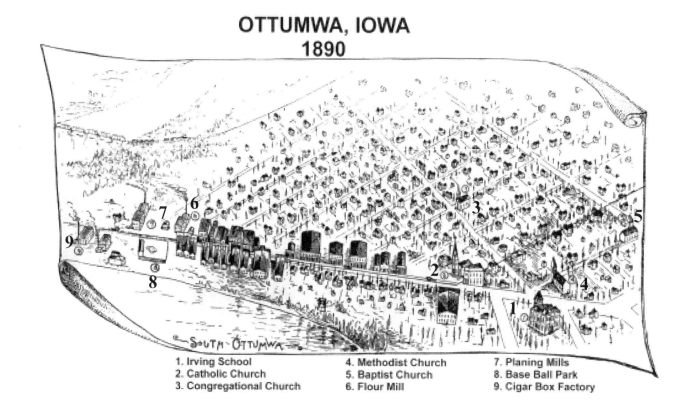

## OTTUMWA, IOWA
## 1890

1. Irving School
2. Catholic Church
3. Congregational Church
4. Methodist Church
5. Baptist Church
6. Flour Mill
7. Planing Mills
8. Base Ball Park
9. Cigar Box Factory

Map of South Ottumwa, 1890. The railroad bridge leading from the north side of town to the Dain (later Deere) Works is at top left. The Market Street Bridge would be just outside the map at lower left. At lower right are old St. Patrick's Church and Irving School (originally known as the south side school). The original channel of the Des Moines River is at lower left. South Ottumwa was a booming economy at the time, with a planing mill, flour mill, and cigar box factory located along Church Street.

Life is like the river, sometimes it sweeps you gently along
and sometimes the rapids come out of nowhere.
--Emma Smith

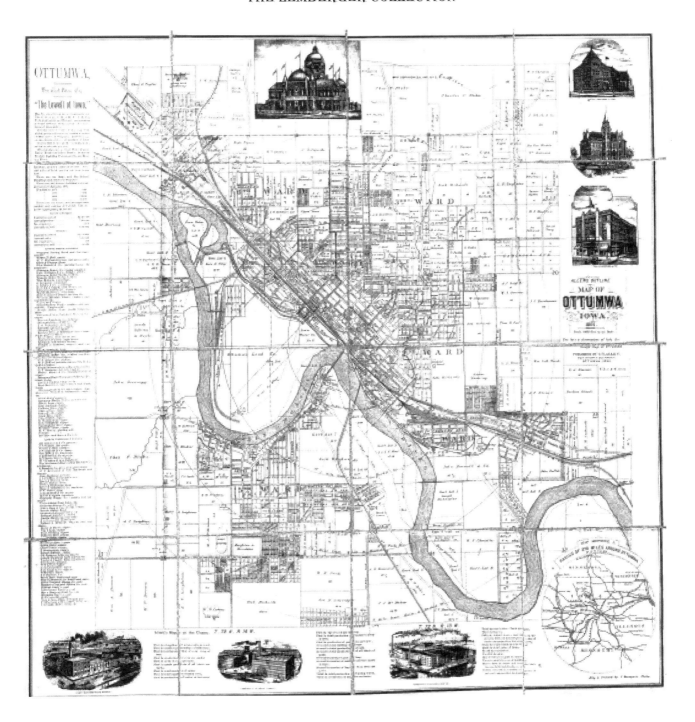

Ottumwa Map from 1891, showing the original looping course of the Des Moines River. The large loop in the river at center left is now the lagoons in Ottumwa Park.

Have you also learned that secret from the river;
that there is no such thing as time? That the river is everywhere at the same time,
at the source and at the mouth, at the waterfall,
at the ferry, at the current, in the ocean and in the mountains,
everywhere and that the present only exists for it,
not the shadow of the past nor the shadow of the future.
--Hermann Hesse

View of downtown Ottumwa and Des Moines River from tower of Lincoln School.
Located on North Court Street, Lincoln School's high tower offered a unique perspective of
downtown. The houses at lower left still stand along North Court Street. The tower visible at
center is the original tower of the Wapello County Courthouse. The courthouse was
completed in 1892 and the tower removed in the 1950s. Washington Street is at lower
right, unpaved and with a car stuck in the mud. The original river channel curves
away in the distance.

Market Street Bridge about 1892. The tree at center is thought to be the big cottonwood where ferries tied up before the bridge was built. The low, marshy area to the right is where the Coliseum (and later Bridge View Center) would be built.

"Oh, Eeyore, you are wet!" said Piglet, feeling him.
Eeyore shook himself, and asked somebody to explain to Piglet
what happened when you had been inside a river for quite a long time.
--A.A. Milne

Flood of 1893, from the tower of Union Depot. A steam locomotive stands in front of the depot. The bridge at center crosses the race (a secondary river channel created for power and water production), while the Market Street Bridge is at upper left. Notice that one span of the Market Street Bridge is under construction, and has been replaced by a temporary span. The houses at top right have been lifted from their foundations by the flood waters and are floating downstream.

Ask the river, where it comes from? You will get no answer.
Ask the river, where is it going? You will get no answer,
because the river lives inside this very moment;
neither in the past nor in the future, in this very moment only!
--Mehmet Murat ildan

If you're not beside a real river, close your eyes,
and sit down beside an imaginary one,
a river where you feel comfortable and safe.
Know that the water has wisdom, in its motion through the world,
as much wisdom as any of us have.
Picture yourself as the water.
We are liquid; we innately share water's wisdom.
— Eric Alan

Flood of 1893, from the tower of Union Depot. This view, taken a little later and from a slightly different angle, shows the Market Street Bridge after the houses swept downstream by the floodwaters knocked out the temporary bridge span.

Market Street Bridge about 1895 – taken from the south side. The tree at center is thought to be the big cottonwood where ferries tied up before the bridge was built. The sidewalk and street appear to be paved with brick, with trolley tracks running down the center of the street. The tower of the Wapello County Courthouse is barely visible behind the poles at left.

---

The river delights to lift us free,
if only we dare to let go.
Our true work is this voyage, this adventure.
— Richard Bach

Railroad bridge, about 1899. This bridge across the Des Moines River connected the north side rail tracks to Dain Manufacturing – later John Deere Ottumwa Works. The tower of the Wapello County Courthouse is visible on the horizon. The smokestack belching vapor is probably that of Hall Candy Company, located on the current site of US Bank. The Wabash Railroad depot is visible at the far (north) end of the bridge. The bridge is now part of the walking trail system.

Sit by a river.
Find peace and meaning in the rhythm of the lifeblood of the Earth.
— Anonymous

17

Men may dam it and say that they have made a lake,
but it will still be a river. It will keep its nature and bide its time,
like a caged animal alert for the slightest opening.
In time, it will have its way; the dam, like the ancient cliffs,
will be carried away piecemeal in the currents.
— Wendell Berry

The steamboat *Columbia* on the Des Moines River near Ottumwa in 1899. Little is known about this vessel, but it appears to be an excursion boat full of passengers, including ladies in elaborate hats. Notice the paddlewheel at the left end of the vessel, under the flags.

This view of two boys standing on ice in the Des Moines River must have been taken after 1899 because Washington School – built in that year as the high school – stands on the horizon. Union Depot is visible in the center. The Market Street Bridge is around the bend of the river to the right, out of sight behind the trees.

I have never seen a river that I could not love.
Moving water . . . has a fascinating vitality. It has power
and grace and associations. It has a thousand colors
and a thousand shapes, yet it follows laws so definite
that the tiniest streamlet is an exact replica of a great river.
— Roderick Haig-Brown

Flood of 1903. This view of Church Street looks from Davis Street toward Five Corners, with the St. Patrick's Church steeple showing behind the poles at center.

A successful man is one that has spent an entire day
on the bank of a river without feeling guilty about it.
— Chinese philosopher

Flood of 1903. A caravan of wagons moves down Church Street, evacuating people and goods from South Ottumwa.

Wild rivers are earth's renegades, defying gravity, dancing to their own tunes, resisting the authority of humans, always chipping away, and eventually always winning.
— Richard Bangs & Christian Kallen

Flood of 1903, taken from near Union Depot. The steam locomotive pushes flood water ahead of its cow-catcher. The Market Street Bridge is in the background; a little of the railroad bridge over the race is also visible.

---

I choose to listen to the river for a while,
thinking river thoughts, before joining the night and the stars.
— Edward Abbey

Who looks upon a river in a meditative hour,
and is not reminded of the flux of all things?
Throw a stone into the stream, and the circles that propagate themselves
are the beautiful type of all influence.
— Ralph Waldo Emerson

Trolley cars on Market Street Bridge. This view from about 1910 is one of the few photographs showing of the south side trolley cars. This is a car on the Ward Street line, just coming off the south end of the Market Street Bridge. Note the filigree ironwork on the bridge, and the tree at right, said to be where ferries tied up before the first bridge was built. The occasion is not known, but the group of men may be forming a color guard for a parade or other ceremony.

© Michael W. Lemberger - Collection

Original hydro dam under construction, 1930s. The original dam was built across the secondary channel (the race), long before the river-straightening project. Though this dam was later extended, the original section remains in place today. The tower of the Wapello County Courthouse is at top right.

A river seems a magic thing.
A magic, moving, living part of the very earth itself.
--Laura Gilpin

Market Street Bridge and cannon.

The big tree at the end of the Market Street
Bridge, said to be where ferries tied up
before the bridge was built. The tree stood
on the riverbank until the 1920s
or early 1930s.

*Above, above left, below left.* The site of the Ottumwa Coliseum in 1932, before construction began. Part of the process of recovering from the Great Depression included the construction of buildings and infrastructure for the public good. The Ottumwa Coliseum and Armory was one of the public works projects funded by the WPA, created to put people back to work while providing lasting projects for the public benefit. The building served as an armory and headquarters for the National Guard unit based in Ottumwa.

These views taken in 1932 show the marshy ground along the river next to the Market Street Bridge, where the Coliseum was to be built. A landfill occupied part of the space (top left). The buildings with sloped roofs (top left) were factories – skylights channeled natural light to workspaces. Some of these buildings were removed before the Coliseum was built, while others remained into the 1960s and 1970s. This area later became the site of Bridge View Center.

Factory buildings near the site of the Coliseum / Armory
(current site of Bridge View Center).

---

I developed my training routine going into my senior year at Jackson State.
I found this sandbank by the Pearl River near my hometown,
Columbia, Miss. I laid out a course of 65 yards or so.
Sixty-five yards on sand is like 120 on turf,
but running on sand helps you make your cuts at full speed.
--Walter Payton

The song of the river ends not at her banks
but in the hearts of those who have loved her.
— Buffalo Joe

Construction crews build the wooden forms to shape concrete pilings to support the
Coliseum structure. Ottumwa High School is across the river in the background.

Building the Coliseum / Armory in 1932 and 1933.

*Above:* Girders go up to form the structure of the Ottumwa Coliseum.

*Left*: Des Moines Steel Co. supplied the girders. Note the size of this one.

*Above*: Block walls go up in the background even as the steel is still being assembled.


*Right*: Setting the Coliseum cornerstone, 1934.

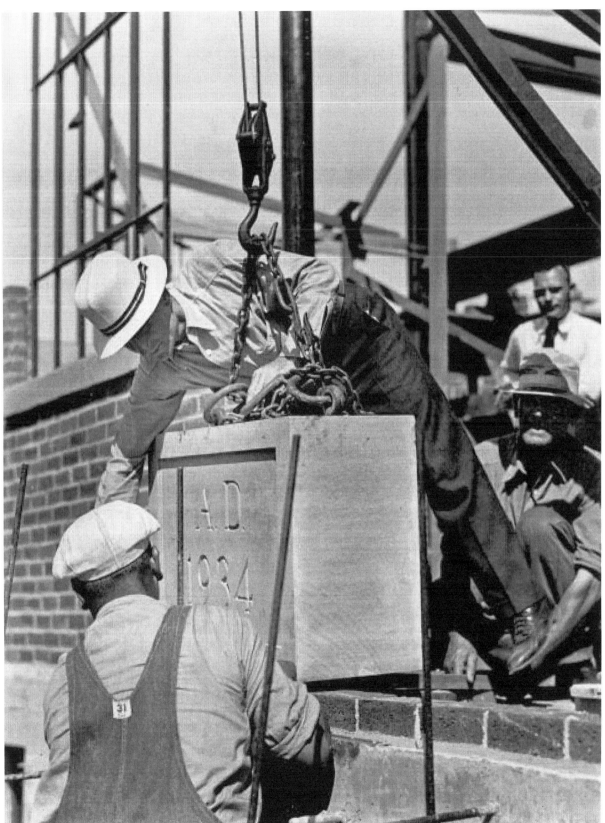

Front facade of the Coliseum building, nearly done -- though doors and steps have yet to be put in place.

How could drops of water know themselves to be a river?
Yet the river flows on.
— Antoine de Saint-Exupery

Another Depression-era public works project – one which still impacts Ottumwans
every day – was the Jefferson Street Viaduct. This view in 1934 shows crews moving dirt in
preparation for starting to build the bridge. Note the old-style dump truck at center left.

Rivers have what man most respects and longs for in his own life—
a capacity for renewal and replenishment,
continual energy, creativity, cleansing.
— John Kauffman

35

*Top left:* Forms are in place, ready for the pouring of support pillars for the Jefferson Street Viaduct. The Wabash Railroad freight house is in the background, 1934.

*Bottom left:* Intersection of Main and Jefferson Streets, showing the bridge pillars under construction near the riverbank, 1934.

*Below:* With pillars in place on both ends of the bridge, work starts in the center of the river. The Coliseum is in the background with factory smoke rising from the buildings behind it. This view was taken from the north side of river looking south.

A temporary bridge was constructed across the river and used to get construction equipment and workers from one riverbank to the other during the construction process. This 1934 view was taken from the south side of the river looking north. The Wabash Depot is at the north end of the bridge, with Ottumwa High School visible on the horizon at top right. Just to the left of the construction crane is the Grand Opera House located at the corner of Main and Jefferson Streets. Wesley Methodist Church and First Lutheran Church are visible at center right.

In this sometimes turbulent world,
the river is a cosmic symbol of durability and destiny;
awesome, but steadfast. In this period of deep national concern,
I wish everyone could live for a while beside a great river.
— Helen Hayes

Workers wheel equipment across a temporary walkway atop the steel framework of the Jefferson Street Viaduct. Note that there is not a hard hat in sight. There are also no nets, safety harnesses, fences or safety rails. The Coliseum is visible in the background.

This view from 1934 shows the pillars of the Jefferson Street Viaduct from ground level. The steel framework of the bridge is in place but decking has not yet been poured.

I started out thinking of America as highways and state lines.
As I got to know it better, I began to think of it as rivers.
Most of what I love about the country is a gift of the rivers. . . .
America is a great story, and there is a river on every page of it.
— Charles Kuralt

If a man fails to honor the rivers,
he shall not gain the life from them.
— The Code of Hammurabi

Some concrete has been laid atop the framework. Note the partially-completed stairs leading down from the viaduct to Jefferson Street. This stairway provided pedestrian access to the street from the bridge. It was not removed until the 1970s. The Grand Opera House at Main and Jefferson Streets is visible in the background, and the tower of First Lutheran Church is on the horizon.

By 1934, the north and south sections of the Jefferson Street Viaduct were about to come together near the south bank of the Des Moines River.

---

Water is fluid, soft, and yielding.
But water will wear away rock, which is rigid and cannot yield.
As a rule, whatever is fluid, soft, and yielding
will overcome whatever is rigid and hard. This is another paradox:
What is soft is strong.
— Lao-Tzu

Rivers are magnets for the imagination,
for conscious pondering and subconscious dreams,
thrills, fears. People stare into the moving water,
captivated, as they are when gazing into a fire.
What is it that draws and holds us?
The rivers' reflections of our lives and experiences are endless.
— Tim Palmer

The dedication of the completed Jefferson Street Viaduct in 1936 included a mass gathering at the south end of the viaduct. The Coliseum is at left, with Ottumwa High School on the horizon at top right.

*Top left:* Old Wapello Street Bridge as it appeared in the 1930s, looking from the north side of the river toward Central Addition at the south end of the bridge.

*Bottom left:* Old Wapello Street Bridge in December 1938, looking north. The mostly wooden bridge spanned the secondary channel (the race), running from Central Addition (what is now Ottumwa Park) to the north side of the river. The Julius Fecht cigar factory and the original waterworks building are visible at center right.

*Below:* Wapello Street Bridge in July 1939. A new concrete and steel span replaced the wooden bridge, running from Central Addition (what is now Ottumwa Park) to the north side of the river. This view was taken from the north end of the bridge looking toward Central Addition. This bridge was replaced by the current Wapello Street Viaduct after the river-straightening project.

Flood of 1944. A family saves their chickens. Note the outhouses at right center. Though the exact location is not known, it is thought to be Sherman Avenue. The 1944 flood was not as destructive or well-known as the 1947 floods; however, the river crested at just over 20 feet and caused extensive damage.

---

*Don't push the river—it flows by itself.*
*— Fritz Perls*

Before 1945 -- Looking northeast over the Des Moines River, showing where the main channel (at bottom) curves around to join the secondary channel (at left) just above the Market Street Bridge. Note the small island near the north bank of the river.
The Coliseum is visible at lower right.

---

Who hears the rippling of rivers will not utterly despair of anything.
— Henry David Thoreau

There is no rushing a river. When you go there,
you go at the pace of the water and that pace
ties you into a flow that is older than life on this planet.
Acceptance of that pace, even for a day,
changes us, reminds us of other rhythms
beyond the sound of our own heartbeats.
— Jeff Rennicke

Metal scrap drive during World War II. Metal donated by Ottumwans to be recycled for the war effort is piled in the parking lot located at the north end of the Market Street Bridge. This view looks south across the river toward the Coliseum and Church Street.

Benton Street Bridge in January 1947. Benton Street connected Central Addition to the north bank of the river, upstream from the Wapello Street Bridge. Photos of the Benton Street Bridge are often misidentified as the old (wooden) Wapello Street Bridge.

Rivers know this:
There is no hurry, we shall get there some day.
— A.A. Milne

Church Street and Jefferson Street Viaduct during the 1947 flood. The water levels during the 1947 flood were actually not the highest water which Ottumwa has experienced, but it was probably the most destructive flood in the city's history because the city experienced two floods within a matter of days. This aerial view shows the south end of the Jefferson Street Viaduct at top, with Victory Park under water in the V formed by the two branches of the viaduct. Carroll Lumber, Mikel's Oldsmobile, and a gas station face Church Street. River water stands in Riverside Park, across Church Street from the businesses. The structure at the top near the end of the bridge is a row of billboards.

This photo shows water levels during the second 1947 flood. The southern end of the Jefferson Street Viaduct is under water and the Coliseum is surrounded by river water. The river level has risen to the deck of the Market Street Bridge (lower right). The original course of the river is marked at right by rows of trees, but water has poured out over the banks and filled Riverside Park (center) and Central Addition (center right).

---

A river does not just happen;
it has a beginning and an end. Its story is written in rich earth,
in ice, and in water-carved stone,
and its story as the lifeblood of the land is filled with colour,
music and thunder.
— Andy Russell

This aerial view of John Deere Ottumwa Works shows the river surrounding the factory. The normal channel of the Des Moines River is at the top of the photograph and is defined by the rows of trees. Vine Street runs along the front of the factory at the bottom of the photo, marked by a row of workers' cars; it too is under water.

---

The face of the river, in time, became a wonderful book . . .
which told its mind to me without reserve,
delivering its most cherished secrets as clearly as if it had uttered them with a voice.
And it was not a book to be read once and thrown aside,
for it had a new story to tell every day.
— Mark Twain

It is with rivers as it is with people:
The greatest are not always the most agreeable
nor the best to live with.
— Henry van Dyke

1947 Flood at John Deere Ottumwa Works. One reason the 1947 flood is considered the worst to hit Ottumwa is that there were two separate floods within a few days. This view of the Vine Street entrance to John Deere Ottumwa Works shows workers wading through river water. Note the white line on the nearest car, at the level of the license plate -- marking the line to which floodwater rose.

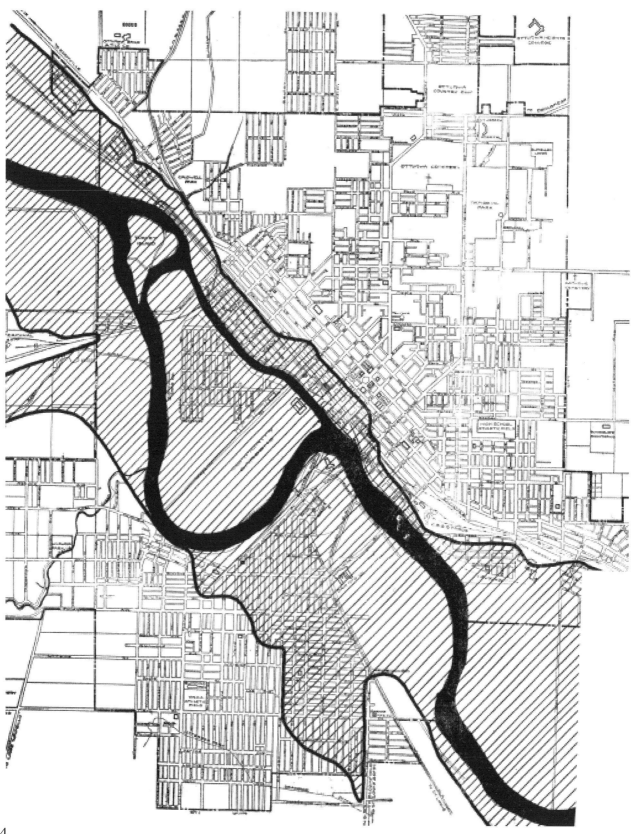

*Above:* Aerial view looking upriver, taken in 1949. This view shows the riverfront before the river straightening project. Market Street Bridge is at bottom, with the main river channel turning off to the left just above the bridge. The straighter channel is the secondary channel, spanned by the original hydro dam and the Wapello Street Bridge. The square basin at center left is a settling basin for the waterworks. Union Depot is at center right and Central Addition (now Ottumwa Park) is at left.

*Left*: Map showing the extent of the 1947 flood. The normal river bed is shown in black; shaded areas show the sections of the city which flooded. One of the reasons why flooding was such a problem for the city is the curves in the river. Each curve slows down the water's flow, and when water can't move quickly down the channel, it spreads out as it slows.

Aerial view of South Ottumwa in the foreground and the north side business district on the far bank of the river, 1949. The Market Street Bridge is at left center, with the Jefferson Street Viaduct in the center and the railroad bridge at right. The Coliseum is visible at the center of the photograph. Victory Park is located in the Y formed by the southern end of the Jefferson Street Viaduct; it was paved over when Highways 34 and 63 were built in the 1960s. At left is the main river channel, with the original hydro dam at far left center, on the secondary channel.

*Right*: Aerial view from the 1940s, before river straightening, looking toward downtown. Turkey Island is visible in the foreground, with the neighborhood which became Marina Gateway at left center. The bridges closest to the camera are the Milwaukee Railroad bridge and Black Hawk Bridge. Central Addition (later Ottumwa Park) is at right center, and a close inspection shows considerable flooding along the main river channel. The secondary river channel is visible through the center of the photo, with the main channel bending off to the right before the two join up again near the Market Street Bridge.

Rivers are places that renew our spirit,
connect us with our past, and link us directly
with the flow and rhythm of the natural world.
— Ted Turner

View of downtown and Des Moines River, 1940s. The secondary channel of the Des Moines River runs through the center, with the main channel breaking off at top left to sweep around Central Addition before the two channels rejoin just above the Market Street Bridge. The original hydro dam is just above the spot where the two channels join. Turkey Island is at top left with the Jefferson Street Viaduct at the bottom of the photo.

View of the Des Moines River from south Ottumwa, 1940s. Turkey Island is at center top, with Richmond Avenue running across the bottom of the photograph. The looping main channel of the river was closed off during the river straightening project and is now the series of lagoons which define Ottumwa Park. The current site of Quincy Place Mall is at left center.

To live by a large river is to be kept in the heart of things.
— John Haines

*Above*: Black Hawk Bridge in about 1948. Black Hawk Bridge was a one-lane span with wooden decking. It carried traffic from Black Hawk Road on the south side of the river to the west end of downtown Ottumwa, near the current site of the Milwaukee Railroad Bridge.

*Top right:* Bicycling across Black Hawk Bridge.

*Bottom right:* The worn wooden decking on Black Hawk Bridge.

The Coliseum was the site of many dances, from the annual Fireman's Ball to sorority balls to events sponsored by Bookin Jewelry. This event was in 1958.

There is no music like a little river's . . .
It takes the mind out-of-doors . . . and . . .
it quiets a man down like saying his prayers.
— Robert Louis Stevenson

You drown not by falling into a river,
but by staying submerged in it.
--Paulo Coelho

Inside the Coliseum, in 1958. The US Army Band, playing in concert to a packed house, was filmed for a special production called *The Big Picture*. Cameras capturing the show are located in the aisles.

Be like a rock in the middle of a river,
let all of the water flow around and past you.
– Zen Saying

Mikels Oldsmobile survived the 1947 flood and stayed in its location on Church Street until the building was replaced by the Holiday Inn and later by the Bridge View Center.

Prompted by the devastation of several floods during the 1940s -- including the double floods of 1947 -- the city began a project to straighten and widen the river and add levees to protect against high water.

The section of the secondary channel upstream from the Wapello Street Bridge has been dredged and widened in this view from July 1957, as the river-straightening project got well underway. Work on the section of the river from Wapello Street to Market Street, including expanding the hydro dam, was yet to come. The dark square in the foreground is a holding pond for the Ottumwa Waterworks. It was eliminated during the expansion of the channel. Turkey Island, the Black Hawk Bridge and the Milwaukee Railroad bridge are near the top of the photograph.

*Above:* Moving dirt to build levees along the river banks.

*Above left and below left:* With the old secondary channel becoming the new main channel, the narrow hydro dam was no longer big enough – so gates were added to span the entire width of the new channel.

With the new dam finished and the new channel open, work began to shut off the flow of the old main channel, turning that section of the river into a series of lagoons which define Ottumwa Park. The lagoons acted as a reservoir in times of high water, and maintained a slow flow in and out so the water wouldn't become stagnant – features which have been lost in recent years. Note the barrel of the cannon at left, above, positioned to look out over the river. It is now in Ottumwa Park.

Levee building near the Coliseum, with the Market Street Bridge in background. 69

All rivers, even the most dazzling, those that catch the sun
in their course, all rivers go down to the ocean and drown.
And life awaits man as the sea awaits the river.
--Simone Schwartz-Bart

Market Street Bridge, looking toward South Ottumwa, in 1962. The elaborate filigree which shows in early photos of the bridge has been removed by this time.

This aerial view in 1963 shows the area around the Ottumwa Coliseum at its most active. Mikels Oldsmobile is gone, but Carroll Lumber is still in operation, with the Holiday Inn booming. Church Street is visible at the bottom of the photo, with the Jefferson Street Viaduct at the top. Victory Park is located in the Y formed by the viaduct's south end.

The river has taught me to listen; you will learn from it, too.
The river knows everything; one can learn everything from it.
— Herman Hesse

The old secondary channel had to be widened considerably to handle the flow of the entire Des Moines River, so the Wapello Street Bridge built in the 1930s was removed and a longer viaduct built to carry Highway 63 traffic over the river.

*Left:* Wapello Street Viaduct under construction.

*Below:* Wapello Street Viaduct shortly after it was completed. This view looks north from the south bank of the river.

© Michael W. Lemberger

*Left and above:* The Jefferson Street Viaduct, 1965.

View from above of the hydro dam 1969.

Jefferson Street Bridge in a night rainstorm, from the intersection of East Main Street and Jefferson Street.

———

If you grew up in the country,
chances are you have fond memories of lazy days
down by a river, creek or pond.
— Darlene Donaldson

View after river straightening. From left: Railroad bridge, Jefferson Street Viaduct, Market Street Bridge. The old main channel of the river has been blocked off at center right and divided into lagoons surrounding the new Ottumwa Park (formerly Central Addition). In the 1960s a new highway was built across south Ottumwa, not far from the river, to carry Highways 63 and 34 through town with ease, rather than by winding through business districts and neighborhoods.

I think the kind of landscape that you grew up in, it lives with you.
I don't think it's true of people who've grown up in cities so much;
you may love a building, but I don't think that you can love it
in the way that you love a tree or a river or the colour of the earth;
it's a different kind of love.
--Arundhati Roy

Highway bridge spanning Church Street just south of the Coliseum / Bridge View site. The embankment on the far side, supporting the bridge, sits atop the old Victory Park. John Deere Ottumwa Works is visible at upper right and the railroad bridge is at top left.

In the 1970s, a new and wider Market Street Bridge was needed to replace the structure which had stood for nearly 100 years. This view from the top of the bridge shows the girders still in place after the decking has been removed. The photographer climbed the slanted end of the bridge, using the rivets as footholds. Hotel Ottumwa is visible on the far side of the river, at left, with First Methodist Church visible just above the bridge and Ottumwa High School on the horizon at top right.

---

A river is the coziest of friends.
You must love it and live with it before you can know it.
— G.W. Curtis

This view in May, 1972 shows the new layout of the riverfront area. From top, the structures on the river are: Wapello Street Viaduct, hydro dam, new Market Street Bridge under construction, Jefferson Street Viaduct, and the railroad bridge. Highways 63 and 34 run along the left of the photo. The Coliseum and Holiday Inn are at left center. Ottumwa Park is at top left. Part of the old river channel is visible as a lagoon by the tennis courts in Riverside Park (left center, across Church Street from the Holiday Inn).

---

If my ship sails from sight,
it doesn't mean my journey ends,
it simply means the river bends.
--Enoch Powell

The river is constantly turning and bending
and you never know where it's going to go
and where you'll wind up. Following the bend in the river
and staying on your own path means that
you are on the right track.
Don't let anyone deter you from that.
--Eartha Kitt

A different angle on the Coliseum area, in May 1972. Market Street Bridge (top right) is under construction. The hydro dam is at top left. The lagoon at center left is now part of the Beach complex. Other landmarks include the Riverside Park tennis courts, the Coliseum, Holiday Inn, Highway 34 / 63, Fareway Grocery, and the Jefferson Street Viaduct.

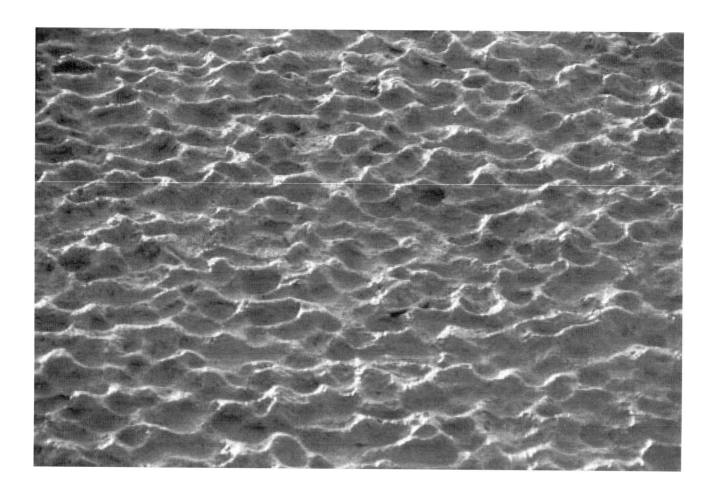

*Above*: Patterns formed in dried mud in the bed of the Des Moines River, photographed from one of the bridges.


*Right*: The Vine Street Bridge, looking across the Des Moines River toward South Ottumwa. John Deere Ottumwa Works is at top, with Highways 34 and 63 between the factory and the river.

© Michael W. Lemberger

© Michael W. Lemberger

© Michael W. Lemberger

*Left:* Vine Street Bridge, looking north across the river.

*Above:* The metal decking of the Vine Street Bridge didn't collect snow and ice during the winter, because precipitation fell through the grating to the river below -- but the rough surface could rattle the driver's teeth if he took the crossing too fast.

Never insult an alligator until after you have crossed the river.
--Cordell Hull

To capture this view, the photographer climbed up the end of the Vine Street Bridge.

Walkway on the Vine Street Bridge with its elaborate iron scrollwork.

Clowning on the walkway of the Vine Street Bridge.

Last remaining span of the Vine Street Bridge. The bridge was closed and removed about 1980. Some of the pier supports are sometimes still visible in the river. Sacred Heart Catholic Church and rectory are at top right.

Abandoned street on Turkey Island, as it appeared in the 1970s.

The Mixmaster -- the eastern intersection of Highways 34 and 63, near John Deere Ottumwa Works. The three-way stop was the site of numerous traffic accidents and was eventually replaced by a roundabout.

This high level aerial photo shows the course of the river as it appeared in 1978. Downtown is at the center of the photo, with Ottumwa Park at top center. From left on the river: Highway 63 bridge leading to the mixmaster, Vine Street Bridge, railroad bridge, Jefferson Street Viaduct, Market Street Bridge, hydro dam, Wapello Street Bridge, Black Hawk Bridge and Milwaukee railroad bridge (connecting across Turkey Island).

*Left:* Planning an event – the Follies – at the Coliseum in 1983.

There are many ways to salvation,
and one of them is to follow a river.
— David Brower

The river in about 1985. Turkey Island is at top left, with the Wapello Street Viaduct, hydro dam, Market Street Bridge, Jefferson Street Viaduct, and the railroad bridge spanning the river. The Coliseum and Holiday Inn are at center left.

*Left*: The Des Moines River in about 1978. Turkey Island is barely visible at top left. The Wapello Street Viaduct, hydro dam, Market Street Bridge, Jefferson Street Viaduct, railroad bridge, and Vine Street Bridge span the river. Other landmarks include the tennis courts in Riverside Park and the Little League fields near the Coliseum.

The Beach, as it appeared in 1993. The lagoons at left and right are part of the original river channel. Riverside Park is at center left, with Highways 34 & 63 running diagonally across the photograph.

---

Rivers run through our history and folklore, and link us
as a people. They nourish and refresh us and
provide a home for dazzling varieties of fish and wildlife and
trees and plants of every sort. We are a nation rich in rivers.
— Charles Kuralt

Flooding in 1993 south and west of the Des Moines River. 1 – Quincy Place Mall; 2 – site of theaters; 3 – site of Applebee's; 4 – site of Vaughn Automotive; 5 – Kmart Plaza; 6 – South HyVee; 7 – Wildwood Drive; 8 – site of WalMart and Menards; 9 – Milwaukee railroad yards; 10 – Blackhawk Road.

A man of wisdom delights in water.
— Confucius

Flood of 1993. When this photograph was taken on July 15, 1993 the river level was extraordinarily high, with flood water lapping at the levees and walls. This view looks south over the Ottumwa Waterworks, showing the hastily-built extra levee intended to protect it from floodwater. A few days before, Des Moines' city waterworks had flooded, leaving the city without water for eleven days. Ottumwa provided tanker trucks of water to Des Moines. The Wapello Street Viaduct is at right; the Burlington Northern depot is at lower left. Note that the railroad tracks are covered by the temporary levee.

*Above:* The Ottumwa Coliseum and Armory.

*Below:* 180-degree panorama of the Coliseum and Holiday Inn shortly before demolition began. Because of the extreme wide angle, Church Street is visible at left AND at right.

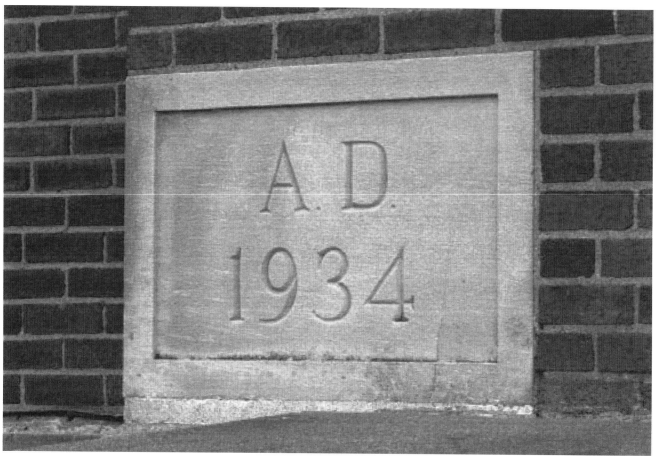

Demolition of the Ottumwa Coliseum begins, February 2005.

*Above:* Design above the door on the west side of the Coliseum.


*Above left:* Cornerstone in place shortly before demolition.

*Below left:* Design detail.

Change not the river, for rocks in the river are good
and are like our problems—
without them we would not know if there was any current.
— Dennis Mapes

Demolition of the Ottumwa Coliseum, February 2005.

March 2005. With the site cleared, dirt moving begins in preparation for the construction of Bridge View Center. Riverside Park and the Beach are visible in the background.

———

There's a river somewhere that flows
through the lives of everyone.
— Roberta Flack

Jefferson Street Viaduct in 2005, showing work
ongoing on the Bridge View Center site, to the left of the bridge.

---

Sometimes we would be staked out in the middle of the river,
several barges tied together.
So we could party.
-- Terry Southern

Sometimes, if you stand on the bottom rail of a bridge
and lean over to watch the river
slipping slowly away beneath you,
you will suddenly know everything there is to be known.
— A.A. Milne

A view which will never again be visible of the Jefferson Street Viaduct, as site preparation continues for construction of the Bridge View Center. Ottumwa High School is in the background. The structure at center right is the remaining portion of the Holiday Inn sign.

*Above and below:* Construction proceeds on Bridge View Center.

The walls of Bridge View Center go up. Hotel Ottumwa, the Wapello County Courthouse, the tower of St. Mary of the Visitation Church, and the tower of First Methodist Church are visible in the background.

If there is magic on this planet, it is contained in water.
— Loren Eiseley

A river, though, has so many things to say
that it is hard to know what it says to each of us.
— Norman Maclean

Bridge View Center under construction, 2005.

Bridge View Center's theater takes shape, 2005.

The first river you paddle runs through the rest of your life.
It bubbles up in pools and eddies to remind you who you are.
— Lynn Noel

*Above and right:* Main entrance to the Bridge View Center, with an architectural nod toward the Ottumwa Coliseum which had occupied the site.

A good river is nature's life work in song.
--Mark Helprin

*Above:* A clock which was used in the Coliseum. Cleaned, restored, and running once more, it is ready for display in Bridge View Center.

*Right*: Chain saw sculpture of Chief Wapello, the county's namesake, looks out over the river from the Bridge View grounds.

*Above*: Fishing in the Ottumwa Park lagoons, 1981.

*Left*: Driftwood log in the Des Moines River, 1978. The Jefferson Street Viaduct and Ottumwa High School are in the background.

Playing at the swimming beach -- one of the lagoons in Ottumwa Park -- in 1972.

---

My idea of a vacation is staying home
and doing short day hikes,
floating the river and things like that.
--Tim Cahill

Driftwood in Ottumwa Park lagoon.

---

I couldn't wait to get on the ice. I couldn't wait to get to practice.
As a kid, I couldn't wait to shoot pucks or play in parking lots,
or play on the river or play on the bay.
--Bobby Orr

Jefferson Street Viaduct during an autumn sunset, 2013. The extreme telephoto lens compresses the view and makes the angles of the bridge appear sharper than they actually are.

---

To connect with the great river we all need a path,
but when you get down there, there's only one river.
--Matthew Fox

Here, on the river's verge, I could be busy for months
without changing my place,
simply leaning a little more to right or left.
--Paul Cezanne

Sunset on the Des Moines River, October 1971.

Sunset reflects from ice on a lagoon in Ottumwa Park, December 2004.

A very long telephoto lens brings many elements together in this photograph taken from
North Court Street near the Wapello County Courthouse:
the Central Park War memorial, The Beach Ottumwa, the hydro dam,
and the Wapello Street Viaduct

The founders of Louis Ville
chose the site because of the bends in the river,
which have provided food and fun, industry and transportation. Since the
town's beginning, the river has been at the heart of the community.

Ottumwa –
a city built on, around, and because of a river.

For more information
about these and other
books, calendars and products,
visit
**www.pbllimited.com**
PBL Limited
P.O. Box 935
Ottumwa Iowa 52501

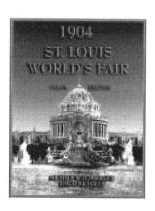

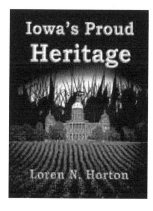

Made in the USA
San Bernardino, CA
05 March 2014